Pampering Polly

Terri Ann King

T.F.H. Publications, Inc.
One TFH Plaza
Third and Union Avenues
Neptune City, NJ 07753

This book has been published with the intent to provide accurate and authoritative information in regard to the subject matter within. While every precaution has been taken in preparation of this book, the publisher and author assume no responsibility for errors or omissions. Neither is any liability assumed for damages resulting from the use of the information herein.

ISBN 0-7938-3108-3

Printed and bound in the United States of America

Printed and Distributed by T.F.H. Publications, Inc.
Neptune City, NJ

Contents

Your Parrot's Needs..5

Making a House a Home 11

Feeding and Nutrition 23

Grooming and Good Health 33

Taming and Training 45

Traveling with Polly..57

Resources 61

Index 63

Your Parrot's Needs

Birds have fascinated people for centuries. Long envious of the birds' ability to fly, humans examined their wing structures and researched many of their gliding characteristics to help design our earliest aircraft. Parrots, once seen as simply undomesticated birds with the ability to mimic words, are now the subjects of intensive research studies. It is now thought that parrots may not mimic after all but actually be able to use words in context. Anyone who has ever owned a parrot that was capable of saying even a few words will probably believe this to be true.

Today the scope of our fascination, admiration, and total captivation with companion parrots continues to grow. As we uncover more about these intelligent creatures sharing our lives, we begin to understand how much there really is to learn about the special relationship between companion birds and humans.

The Pet-Owner Relationship

There was a time when bird keeping was as simple as putting a pet in a wire cage and feeding it seeds for the rest of its life. Sometimes, if a bird was lucky, it would receive a little more attention and possibly a mirror or a food treat. Only recently has the complex relationship between birds and humans been truly discovered. For this reason I refer to those parrots that share our lives as companion birds rather than pet birds. They are far more than pets—and they demand and need so much more than just seeds to make them happy. Today's companion bird owners dedicate more time, money, and effort toward pampering their feathered friends than ever before. To make things easier, there is a constant stream of new products to help us keep our birds healthy and happy.

Your gentle, loving care is the best way to start pampering your companion bird.

Fortunately, whenever we pamper our birds we also reap the benefits of sharing our lives with an appreciative, contented, and healthy companion.

Meeting Physical, Mental, and Emotional Needs

Until recently many bird owners felt that the most important aspect of bird keeping was to meet physical needs such as food and water. Only after these needs were met did owners even think about the mental and emotional requirements that companion parrots might have. Often, unless there was a specific problem behavior such as feather plucking or screaming, the mental and emotional needs of companion birds were not considered at all.

These physical, mental, and emotional needs are equally important, especially because one will often have a direct effect on the other. For example, if a companion parrot is bored because it has nothing to do in the confines of its cage all day long, it may well begin screaming or feather plucking. The mental need for stimulation thus manifests itself in such an emotional behavior. You can see how, in time, a condition such as feather plucking could have adverse physical effects if the bird gets an infection or loses blood from extreme self-picking. This is no idle problem—feather plucking is quite common among caged birds, and seemingly more prominent among species such as African Greys. Cockatoos are known rather notoriously as being screamers; indeed, I know of 11 cockatoos right now awaiting new homes after being returned by disappointed owners. The fact that these types of parrots have these particular behavioral problems is often no accident, nor is it a "problem" of the species. These parrots are highly intelligent creatures. African Greys need mental stimulation to appease their curious, intellectual minds, so it is no wonder that when

Toys will likely be an important part of your parrot's life, but they should never replace personal attention and interaction.

faced with a boring situation they resort to other types of stimulation, as destructive as this may be. Cockatoos are known as affectionate birds, so when they lack the proper environment to keep them contented they often resort to screaming in a desperate attempt for attention.

In the past, owners were often discouraged from certain species of companion birds because of behaviors such as feather plucking, screaming, and biting. This is not only unfair, it is also unfortunate for both bird and owner. No bird should be stereotyped with a certain personality type, because so much of its personality depends on its owner's. A companion bird also develops according to the environment it is in, which is encouraging news to owners who feel that they are "stuck" with a problem bird and have no recourse but

A clever Amazon parrot will benefit from the stimulation involved in prying a food treat out of a toy.

to live with it or give it away. We now know that there are many things we can do as owners to create an environment conducive to happy, healthy birds. This is not to say that you will never encounter a bird with a behavioral problem. But many of these problems can be corrected, eliminated, or prevented altogether by learning a few ways to adjust yourself and your bird's environment.

All parrots have different needs, but a parrot that feels lonely or neglected may resort to feather plucking.

Birdaholics Anonymous

Many owners find themselves with multiple birds because they think that birds have to be around other birds. This is not necessarily true. However, it can be a positive experience for both owners and birds when two or more parrots share a household. Even if particular species don't quite get along to the point of actually housing together, most parrots are so gregarious in nature that they do enjoy being around other birds. This is true in the wild and can also be true in the confines of your home.

There are times when having and housing multiple birds can become a serious problem. Birdaholics, those who live with too many birds, face a host of problems. Keeping more birds than you can realistically handle is as serious as any addiction that prevents you—and those around you—from enjoying your full potential as friend, caretaker, or family member. So it is important to determine how many birds you can realistically care for without causing them or yourself undue stress or lowered standards of care. In short, if you often feel as if you are somehow denying your bird optimum time and attention by having to split your affection too many ways, you might be a birdaholic.

The decision to keep multiple birds should be carefully considered, especially if your free time is limited.

Owning more than one bird can have rewards as well as limitations, however. The important thing is to know when you have reached a reasonable limit, which may vary from person to person. It could differ depending on the particular species of birds you decide to live with. One Umbrella cockatoo could demand so much of your time and attention that even one other bird would be considered too many. Other birds, such as conures and Rose-breasted cockatoos, are often more independent, allowing you as an owner to keep more than one or two. But it is important to remember that each of your birds is an individual and will have its own particular needs. Realize that every bird you have will need as much personal attention as you can spare, and that each additional bird will automatically reduce the amount of attention that all your companion parrots will receive. Having understood this,

Time spent reading, relaxing, or even watching television with your bird will be much appreciated.

it remains the discretion of each person to determine what number of birds works best for his or her lifestyle.

The needs of companion birds vary as widely as the parrots themselves, but you will find that all birds require several basic things in order for them to be physically, mentally, and emotionally healthy. First of all, they need a proper place to call home—a place where they can relax and enjoy some privacy. They also need a healthy and varied diet. Companion birds must be groomed, and they should also have access to quality health care in the form of a competent avian veterinarian. They need to be tamed, of course, but they also need to be provided with training and guidance so that they are sociable, agreeable companions. Once these basic needs are met, there are still many other ways to ensure that your avian companion is healthy, happy, and fulfilled. You will find that companion birds are really not much different than any one of us in their wishes and needs. They just want to enjoy the best life possible. If you are an experienced companion bird owner, you are already aware that birds need and want your love, care, and an extra bit of attention. If you are a new bird owner just beginning the wonderful experience of sharing your life with a companion bird, you may be pleasantly surprised at how rewarding it can be to pamper your parrot in style.

Making a House a Home

The big day has arrived, and you are about to bring "Polly," your new parrot, home. You have probably gone to a great deal of trouble to find out what kind of bird would work best for you, perhaps you have checked out dozens of potential pets before deciding on your particular parrot. Regardless of whether this is your first bird or one of several you already live with, you should know that the first step is to provide it with adequate housing. Fortunately for today's bird owners, there are cages to please every bird—and every owner. Modern birdcages come in all shapes, sizes, and colors—it is simply a matter of sorting it all out to decide which cage setup is right for your parrot. From there, it is relatively easy to make that house a home.

Basic Housing Requirements

There are many different ideas of what constitutes basic housing requirements for companion birds. For smaller species, the cage should have proper bar spacing to ensure that your bird can't become caught between the bars. Likewise, a larger parrot should have wider bar spacing to ensure that it can have visual stimulation beyond the cage. Many standards have been suggested for cage size for particular species. Although I agree with the minimum standard that stipulates that every bird should have adequate room for wing flapping, climbing, and exercising, I hesitate to adopt any standard for a maximum size. In short, I believe that every cage you house your bird in should be as large as you can possibly afford; of course, within monetary and room size limitations. There are many good reasons for housing your bird in the largest cage possible. Larger cages allow room for

A large parrot like a Scarlet macaw requires a well-constructed and spacious cage, which may not be possible in all homes.

toys, sleeping quarters (if desired), treat dispensers, and tubs for bathing. However, the number one reason for housing your bird in the largest cage possible is because no matter how spacious the new home is, it is still a lot smaller than the jungle, or the bird's natural habitat. And even though your bird may be a handraised baby that has never known the wilds of its native habitat, it still instinctively needs and enjoys the freedom to explore its environment.

Once the maximum cage size is determined, other decisions must still be made. As has already been noted, bar spacing is important. For safety reasons it is always essential that the bar spacing remain correct regardless of the large size of the overall cage. This is especially important for the smaller species of birds such as inquisitive conures and cockatiels. New cage buyers often overlook another consideration with the bars, but it is one that many birds consider extremely important. Bars on most cages are either horizontal, vertical, or both. Some people recommend that bars should be one way or the other, depending on the species. Certain birds like to climb and so need horizontal bars. Others would rather remain lower on their perches, and vertical bars allow them greater visibility for looking out through the cage. I have found that to really pamper your avian companion—regardless of what kind of parrot it is—a cage with both horizontal and vertical bars (varying on all sides) works best. Many birds enjoy climbing to the top of the cage and then sliding down the vertical bars like firemen. I have watched both conures and cockatoos do this with endless enjoyment. They certainly miss the fun when they are placed in a travel cage with only horizontal bars.

Another consideration is whether to get a cage with a dome top or to get one with a flat top, which often comes with a play area outside atop the cage. Again, it is important to consider both your situation and

A cage should be equipped with a number of accessories; a treat clip holds a tasty millet spray in place for a blue parakeet.

your bird's. For active, climbing, and smaller parrots such as conures and cockatiels, which love climbing to the highest point and surveying their world, the dome top cages are probably preferred. Larger birds such as macaws and cockatoos often seem more willing to give up the dome top in favor of the play top outside of the cage where they can spend much of their time. In short, if a bird is going to be outside of its cage quite a bit—which I recommend, especially for the larger parrots—then the play top cages are a wonderful idea. Of course, even the smaller birds enjoy time out of the cage, but it is easier to allow them that privilege by installing a perch on the outside of their cage somewhere near the top. They then feel free to perch outside or climb around their dome top.

A final consideration has to do with the floor of the cage: should you have a

Multiple birds should each have their own cage, but they can spend time together in a larger cage or on a playstand.

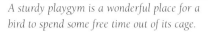

A sturdy playgym is a wonderful place for a bird to spend some free time out of its cage.

grate at the bottom or allow the bird access to the cage floor? This is an important consideration, especially because many species enjoy walking around on the ground searching for food in the wild. Rose-breasted cockatoos, for example, forage along the ground in fields and on roadsides searching for seeds and grains in their homeland of Australia. My own two rosies spend a lot more time than I would prefer exploring the floor of their cage. At first I tried to accommodate them by lining the floor with walnut shells and allowing them access to the bottom of the cage. I have since reconsidered and have decided that for the sake of cleanliness and their own health, I would have to reinstall the bottom grate to keep them from walking around on the bottom and eating soiled foods. I compensate by allowing them time out of the cage to explore our tiled family room. At times I will even hide treats around the room so they can experience "foraging" for

A cage fitted with wheels will allow you to roll it outside, where most birds will enjoy the fresh air and sunshine.

food (I limit it to supervised time out). In general, I feel that it is better to keep a bottom grate in the cage so birds will be discouraged from spending unsupervised time on the floor below, where they could ingest things harmful to their health.

Once you have ensured that your avian companion has the most wonderful home it deserves, take time to consider your own needs. Choose a cage color that enhances your home as well as your bird's coloration. Unless your bird has a particular aversion to a given color, you can generally choose one to your liking. There are also cages shaped like houses and those beautifully crafted of oak or hardwood to compliment your home as an elegant piece of furniture. These often come equipped with acrylic siding, air filtration systems, and full spectrum lighting to minimize your work and maximize your parrot's good health.

Ease of maintenance is a critical design element to consider in a cage. Many modern designs have removable trays at the bottom and easy access feeder doors, as well as skirts to catch food that would otherwise land on the floor. Stainless steel cages are fairly easy to keep clean and can be fitted with feeder dishes that attach to the outside of the cage to maximize cage space and eliminate messes from droppings. Hanging water bottle dispensers can often prevent contaminated drinking water. Be certain to provide your bird with a bowl for splashing and dunking if it enjoys these things. Many cages come with birdproof latches. Some even have interchangeable arch and playpen tops to add a little variety to your parrot's life. Whatever you decide, pick a design that works for you as well as for your bird.

Beyond House and Home

Now that you've decided on a cage for your bird, you can go about making the house a home. This is not unlike moving into your first house and designing it to suit your own personal preferences. Be prepared to move items several times before you and your bird are both satisfied with the layout. Don't worry—Polly will be more than happy to let you know if the arrangement is satisfactory or not. Getting there is half the fun.

I recommend that several different perches be installed in the cage. Concrete perches, conveniently located by the food and water dishes where they are likely to be utilized, are helpful in ensuring that your bird's nails remain trimmed. Because most birds rub their beaks to clean them after eating, concrete perches near the food dish also help your bird to keep its beak filed and in great operating

A pair of Rose-breasted cockatoos shares an acrylic-and-concrete combination swing.

order. Rope perches are also a nice touch; I have found that placing these a little higher up on the cage allows your bird to enjoy a great view, a little swinging action similar to a high swaying tree limb, and

Plain dowel perches are fine, but perches of varying size and material will give your bird's feet some relief and exercise.

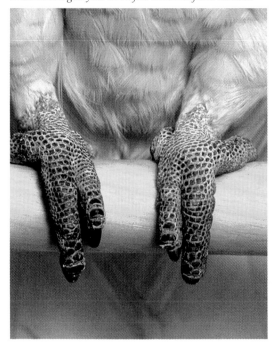

a comfortable place to rest its feet. Rope perches also provide something for the bird to pull at, and they can preen each small strand that comes loose. Be prepared to replace these from time to time—but not before your companion parrot has had a chance to shred the rope into hundreds of beautifully preened strands. Finally, natural wood perches are a great addition to any bird's home. They provide stable footing and allow the bird something to gnaw and chew on. A few perches of varying diameters are welcomed by most birds because they simulate the different branches birds would have access to in the wild. Natural wood perches of varying sizes also help ensure that your bird learns to grip and perch properly (and they are great foot exercisers).

Crock dishes made with bird-safe materials and glazing are excellent for both food and

Ceramic crocks come in many sizes and colors; in addition, such non-porous dishes inhibit the growth of bacteria.

water. These dishes are easy to clean and are heavy enough that they can't be picked up or pushed around by your bird as readily as lightweight plastics. Also, birds can't chew these types of bowls. They are even available in covered or domed versions so your bird's food and water don't get contaminated as quickly. A wide variety of designs and colors are available. Stainless steel feeding dishes offer another alternative. Not only are they lightweight and easy to clean, you may notice that even finicky eaters can be encouraged to take an interest in food when they can see themselves in the bottom of the bowl!

A cage cover will help your bird feel protected as well as allow it to get plenty of restful sleep at night.

Extra Treats

Once the cage is suitably outfitted with the essential equipment, you can go a step further to indulge your parrot. Just as many of us enjoy fresh flowers in our home, your bird will appreciate those days that you offer fresh cut branches and leaves for its chewing pleasure. These natural treats can be woven through the cage bars, preferably on the top of the cage, where birds delight in climbing up to chew their prize. Just be certain the branches and leaves are from bird-safe and

Toxic Plants: Not For Snacking

Sometimes, birds and plants don't mix. Although live plants can be a great way to enhance your bird's "habitat," many plants can make your bird sick, and some can kill. Don't take a chance. (A complete list is available from the ASPCA/National Animal Poison Control Center.)

Aloe vera
Amaryllis (bulbs)
Apple (seeds)
Apricot (pits)
Asparagus fern
Avocado
Azalea
Baby's breath
Bird of paradise
Bittersweet
Bleeding heart
Boxwood
Calla lily
Caladium
Castor bean
Cherry (bark, leaves, pits)
Christmas cactus
Christmas rose
Chrysanthemum
Clematis
Corn plant
Crocus (bulbs)
Daffodil (bulbs)
Daisy
Dieffenbachia
Dogwood
Elephant ear
English ivy
Foxglove
Geranium
Gladiola
Hibiscus

Holly
Hyacinth
Hydrangea
Impatiens
Iris
Jasmine
Lily of the valley
Marijuana
Mistletoe (berries)
Morning glory
Narcissus
Onion
Peace lily
Peach (leaves and pit)
Philodendron
Plum (leaves and pit)
Poinsettia
Poison ivy
Poppy
Primula
Privet
Rhododendron
Rhubarb (leaves)
Snapdragon
Sweet pea
Tiger lily
Tobacco
Tomato (stem, leaves, green fruit)
Tulip
Verbena
Weeping fig
Yucca

non-poisonous trees. Eucalyptus, citrus branches, and palm fronds are widely accepted and should be used if available. Otherwise, check your local plant and tree selection and find what is healthy and might be enjoyed by your parrot. Dandelion and other unsprayed or untreated plants are also considered a special treat by most birds.

Even if you house your parrots in outside aviaries, they still enjoy a daily selection of fresh greenery. Because there is more room in an aviary than a cage, you may be able to put entire trees within the confines of the enclosure. Potted plants and trees work best for those aviaries that are raised with grated floors. Add a mist system for hot afternoons, and your bird will find itself in a tropical paradise.

Birds enjoy natural trees so much that many owners have fashioned actual natural tree branches into play areas for their avian companions outside of the cage. If you go to local bird markets, you can usually find a variety of these perching trees for sale in all different sizes, shapes, and styles. Birds love this particular kind of play area. To build your own, first find a large section of untreated bird-safe tree limbs with several branches going in different directions that can be used for perching and climbing. Cut a large limb off at the base and wash it thoroughly. Center the cut bough upright in a large clay pot used for planting patio trees or large shrubs. The limb can be fastened to the bottom of the pot by installing a large wood screw and washer through the bottom drain hole of the container. Next, fill the pot almost completely with sand, allowing a few inches at the top so that you can pour concrete or mortar mix in to secure the base of the limb. Now your birds have a wonderful climbing and perching "tree" of natural wood. A similar play gym can be made out of plastic water pipe, which is easily cut and can be fitted any way you wish to design the "branches." Although this is lighter and therefore more portable to move from room to room, a truly pampered parrot may prefer a natural wood play area. Other products available include play towers with "branches" that can be rearranged to provide your parrot with a new play area whenever you desire to do so. This is helpful in preventing boredom and may even help prevent excessive territoriality in young maturing parrots.

A Sun conure is thrilled with its special treat—a fresh-cut bough from a pesticide-free grapefruit tree.

Some birds prefer more protection and privacy than others; special covered perches and roosting tents can help.

Special Needs for Special Birds

At some point, many owners are faced with caring for a disabled or older bird. It is a sad fact that not all birds are born perfect, but an even sadder fact that these birds are sometimes overlooked as companions. In fact, many disabled and older birds make wonderful companions. They do, however, often need special help to ensure that they are happy and healthy. For example, many birds have problem feet that either were deformed at birth or perhaps bitten off by a sibling when they were still in the nest. It is necessary to ensure that these little guys have somewhere to rest other than a hard wood or cement perch, or even a swaying rope. A corner platform covered with some kind of carpeting works great as a place for allowing older birds or those birds with sore, tired feet a place to rest. They certainly seem to appreciate it, especially if the platform is placed a little bit higher up in the cage, where they can survey their kingdom. Even birds without disabilities enjoy these corner platforms. Another way to pamper your bird, one that is especially appreciated by some of the smaller species, is to provide a hanging tent-like structure made of cloth that they can crawl into to hide from the world. These tents have been manufactured in many different sizes and colors; it may take some experimentation to find the right one for your bird. For example, my Sun conure would not go anywhere near a yellow tent but would gladly dive into a dark green one. My Rose-breasted cockatoos prefer a dark purple one. Some people believe that it's most effective to make the hideaways the same color as the bird for best results. But different birds will have different preferences; although my Blue-crown conure doesn't like any sort of tent at all, he does enjoy spending his nights on a carpet-covered corner platform. He had a broken hip before I got him and his feet were always red and swollen on the bottom—especially the one that bore all the weight. Since he has had the corner platform to sleep on, his feet have healed and he can still enjoy his concrete, wood, and rope perches during the day.

Many birds are shy by nature and most enjoy their privacy at least once in a while during the day. Almost all birds enjoy a quiet, darkened cage to sleep in at night. If you have a bird that is especially shy, nervous, or even just intensely private, it is helpful to provide a partial cage cover. Design one that can be dropped over one or two sides of the cage during the times when your parrot seems to want or need a little extra security. Nervous or shy birds usually take comfort in a cage packed with toys. It can help to put several hanging toys around the timid bird's favorite resting perch, platform, or tent so that it can hide among them to feel more secure.

Older or handicapped birds also appreciate having easy-to-grip perches mounted throughout the cage as well as easy access to their food and water bowls. My male cockatoo, Jake, had a broken

Essential Cleaning Supplies

Yes, cleaning is a chore. But it's a matter of health, so it must be done regularly and thoroughly. Having the proper tools and supplies—and keeping them in a convenient location—can make things easier, however.

- Paper towels: no job is too big—or too small—for a decent roll of paper towels. Keep these handy at all times.

- Cloth towels: old terrycloth towels are great for some cleanups, as well as for protecting your clothing and furniture from bird droppings.

- Newspapers: as cage liners or floor coverings, there's nothing as basic or efficient as newspapers; stick to black-and-white pages only.

- Cleaning solution: for day-to-day cleanups using a spray bottle, a simple soap-and-water solution should be used. Avoid anything with fumes, which will harm your bird.

- Disinfectant: for weekly or monthly cleaning jobs, a bleach solution (one cup bleach to one gallon of water) or specially purchased bird cleaning disinfectant should be used to thoroughly soak cages and accessories. These items should then be air-dried before your bird has contact with them.

- Brushes: an assortment of brushes will make it easier to scrub cages, perches, and other accessories.

- Vacuum: a hand-held vacuum dedicated to your bird's area will save you an enormous amount of time picking up bird and food debris.

left leg before we brought him home and, although it has healed nicely, he still can't seem to grasp food in his foot like most other parrots. He watches the female cockatoo, Sheila, nonchalantly eating food gripped firmly in her foot and tries unsuccessfully to do the same. Noticing this dilemma, my husband carved a very shallow indented "bowl" from a piece of a eucalyptus branch. He fastened the branch to the side of the cage next to Jake and Sheila's food dish. In no time at all, Jake was contentedly placing food he picked up from the dish onto his indented branch and eating from that. Though Sheila uses the carved-out branch occasionally, Jake uses it all the time. Designs like this can help other birds that have trouble holding food or treats such as peanuts. The simple shallow

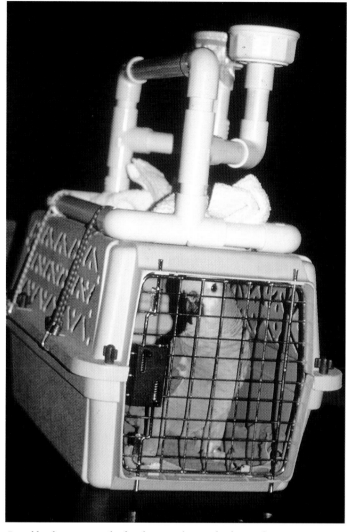

Portable playgyms can be fitted to travel cages for fun on the run.

branch may also be appreciated by African Greys, cockatoos, and other species that simply enjoy eating "off the ground" as they do in the wild.

Special birds have special needs. However, almost any need can be met, which should allow your parrot to live a long and comfortable life, regardless of its age or limitations. It is as easy to pamper an elderly or handicapped bird as it is to fuss over any other avian companion, and you will find the rewards to be well worth your efforts.

Feeding and Nutrition

B irds, like humans, are what they eat. There is probably no better way to ensure that your bird is happy and healthy than to provide it with a good diet throughout its life. Avian nutrition is constantly being researched, and new products allow bird owners to provide their companion birds with tasty, healthy, and fun-to-eat foods more conveniently than ever before.

Eating healthy allows a companion bird to live a longer, less stressful life than it would enjoy in the wild. Birds in their natural environment would spend a large part of their day foraging for food. When we provide for all of their nutritional needs, we are ensuring that they get a healthy and varied diet, but we are also eliminating the natural means of exercise and mental stimulation they would normally get by searching for their dinner. It is probably just as important to give birds this stimulation as it is to give them proper nutritional foods. Fortunately, this is not a problem—you simply have to provide your birds with an opportunity to work for their food. This can be done in any number of ways, but most certainly through different types of treat dispensers that encourage birds to think in order to be able to retrieve the food items. Other methods of simulating the type of foraging that your parrot might do in the wild include hiding treats, offering nuts or seeds still in the shell, and hanging greens in places where the bird must climb to retrieve them. In time, you will think of many fun games and methods to make your bird work for its food. Recently, my mother discovered that her Indian Ringneck loves spaghetti. Rather than putting the long strands in a bowl, she wove them in and out of the cage bars where they could dangle freely and amuse her bird. Try to think of creative ways to get your own reluctant or bored parrot to enjoy its dinner. But always remember that a supply of healthy food, such as pellets, should be available at all times without having a bird work for it. There may be times when your bird doesn't feel like working for its dinner, and this should be respected. Further, a companion bird should never have to work for water. A fresh, clean, and adequate supply of water should be readily available at all times. This having been said, you can use your imagination to make mealtime fun for your bird and treat your parrot by providing a wide variety of foods in a wide variety of ways.

Basic Nutritional Needs

There are many books detailing avian nutritional needs, and I encourage every bird owner to read them and to keep up with current findings. There are, however, simple ways to help ensure that our birds are eating right. Providing your bird with a manufactured diet such as pelleted food is probably the easiest way to make sure it is getting all of the essential vitamins and minerals; these diets are balanced and provide

Your bird relies on you for its every need—including a regular supply of fresh and nutritious foods.

If given the choice, many birds would eat seeds alone; however, a varied and balanced diet is critical to your bird's health.

all of the nutritional needs necessary for optimum health. (Note: this does not mean that your parrot should be fed only pellets—a varied diet is always best.) Many products are being continuously re-evaluated and updated as research shows that birds either need something added or prefer different tastes, colors, or shapes. A good rule of thumb is to provide your birds with a dish of pellets at all times so that when it is hungry it can always go to the dish for a healthy snack. Fun-to-eat hanging treat sticks, seed balls, and cake-like squares are also available as part of a manufactured diet. These can be given along with, or often in place of, pellets. One innovative treat combines popcorn with seeds and pellets into a delectable ball of fun. Another favorite hanging treat consists of cholla cactus stuffed with peanuts in a delicious bar. Tasty mineral blocks in a variety of flavors are also available to aid nutritional needs and entice your parrot into trimming its beak. These products are usually a welcome addition to any diet.

Think Green

Although manufactured diets generally ensure that your bird is getting balanced, healthy nutrition in every bite, it is still necessary to give your birds fresh fruits and vegetables every day. An easy way to remember which greens are healthiest is to associate color with nutrition; as a general rule, dark green vegetables are usually more nutritious than light green vegetables. Fresh carrots are also very good for your bird's health; parrots usually love the greens of the carrot tops best. Vegetables are probably more essential to

Although captive birds lack the physical stimulation of finding food in the wild, there are ways to make mealtimes more exciting.

your bird's health than fruit, but your bird certainly will appreciate the occasional apple, grape, banana, and citrus treat. Be certain to wash all vegetables and fruits thoroughly and remove skins, seeds, and cores. In a hurry? Frozen vegetables can be thawed and offered on those busier days. Ideally, you should select vegetables and fruits that are fresh, local, and have been organically grown.

If your bird is not interested in a bowl of fresh veggies, try clipping them to the top of its cage for a change.

To really pamper your parrot, try growing and sprouting your own greens and vegetables.

Seed Appeal

Although seeds, which are rather fattening and less nutritious than other foods, have recently been discouraged as a main staple in your bird's diet, they can still be an important supplemental food. Seeds provide some nutrition; moreover, a certain amount of fat is necessary in any diet. They also provide a fun way to exercise and stimulate your companion birds, which will certainly enjoy cracking open seeds to get to the good stuff

No one food should dominate your bird's diet—a mixture of seeds, pellets, dried fruits, nuts, and pasta provides variety, taste, and nutrition.

within. Plus, birds just love seeds. In their natural habitat most birds would include seeds and grains as part of their diet; therefore, this natural food should not be entirely denied to them in captivity. Seeds should be limited, however, because many birds will not eat anything else if they have seeds available as an alternative. Large and small millet spray is usually welcomed by birds, but can also become the preferred meal, so it should also be limited to the occasional treat.

Supplements

Keeping a manufactured diet available at all times, offering fruit and vegetables daily, and using a seed mixture as an occasional treat is usually a good way to ensure that your bird is eating properly. As a rule, extra vitamins and supplements are not necessary with a manufactured diet. Keep in mind, however, that egg-laying hens, older birds, and birds of certain species may have special dietary needs. Do your research if you feel you have such a situation.

Specialties

There is no end to the different specialty foods you can provide for your bird. In general, if you like it and it is healthy for you, your bird will probably enjoy it as well. There are many commercial foods on the market for the busy bird owner, some that allow you to simply add water and microwave. But if you have a bit of time, it is fairly simple to make your own "secret recipes." There are even a few avian cookbooks available to assist you in making healthy recipes for your favorite feathered friend. In time, you will probably be able to write your own.

Pasta, beans, rice, and barley are the four key ingredients for making delicious treats for your bird. Preparation and serving is simple, especially if you make it in bulk and then freeze it in individual packages that can be thawed as needed. Begin by getting as many kinds of beans as you can find (I usually buy a bean soup mixture with anywhere from 9 to 15 different types of beans). Soak these beans for a few hours and rinse them several times to remove any dirt. Then boil them along with the barley, and add rice a little later. Add the pasta last because it cooks the fastest. As soon as the pasta begins to soften, remove the entire mixture from the heat and rinse quickly in cold water. Drain thoroughly and put the cooled mixture immediately into plastic bags—snack bags work best. Then place the individual snack bags into one large freezer bag and freeze. When it is time to pamper your bird with a healthy treat, simply remove a snack bag from the freezer and thaw it in a bowl of hot water. You can give it to your birds as is or add chopped greens, thawed frozen mixed vegetables, or even a scoop of your bird's favorite seed mixture. Making it yourself is not only less expensive, it also ensures that the food is free of salt and preservatives.

Depending on how much time you have, you may wish to grow your own herbs, sprouts, and natural bird food. Do-it-yourself kits are available at most pet stores and bird shops, or you can try your hand at growing organic vegetables in your own backyard.

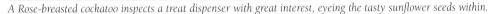

A Rose-breasted cockatoo inspects a treat dispenser with great interest, eyeing the tasty sunflower seeds within.

Fresh water must be provided daily; you may need to experiment with different dishes and drinkers to see which works best with your bird.

Snacks

Parrots also appreciate special snacks from time to time. Fortunately, there are some smart snacks that allow you to satisfy your bird's cravings and still keep its diet relatively nutritious. Try offering your bird some chunky peanut butter on a spoon or on a whole-wheat cracker.

A Double Yellow-headed Amazon digs into a juicy honeydew melon treat—seeds and all.

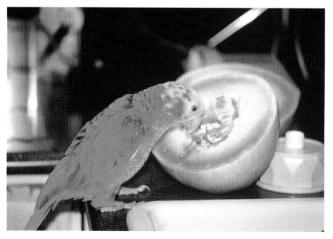

Peanut butter can be fattening, so use in moderation if you have a parrot prone to obesity. Another greatly enjoyed treat is freshly squeezed orange juice, especially with the pulp. Your bird may even enjoy sipping this right out of your glass in the morning. Unsweetened cereal and bran flakes with raisins are other fun treats that birds enjoy crunching up or dunking in their water bowls. Even a crust of pizza with just a little topping is a satisfying snack. Unsalted pretzels are loads of fun to crush or dunk. Please note that there are certain foods that should never be given to parrots—things such as chocolate, coffee, or alcoholic beverages. Even some foods that would seem healthy are to be avoided, avocados in particular, which are considered harmful for birds. Keep a list of which foods can be harmful for your parrots and don't include them in the diet—even as snacks or treats.

Picky Eaters

Sooner or later, most parrot owners will find themselves stuck with a picky eater. If you adopt or inherit an older bird, you may initially have trouble getting it to try different foods. Handfed babies that have been offered a large variety of foods after they have been weaned are usually less resistant to trying new foods; however, there are exceptions. Finally, some birds just

Small and large birds alike relish millet spray, which is millet seeds left on the stem.

seem to be born seedaholics and may only eat sunflower seeds. So how do you encourage a picky eater to try other foods?

Patience. When you offer new foods, be prepared to waste a good portion of the offerings for

A food that is healthy for you is probably fine for your bird; however, be particularly cautious about salt, fat, and sugar.

days, sometimes weeks, before your bird even tries them. Some birds will ignore the new food; others will take one experimental bite and then rub their beaks frantically on a nearby perch in total distaste. Although there will be healthy foods that your bird may never learn to truly enjoy, there are ways to increase the chances that an interest will be taken in at least trying them, which is more than half the battle; if your parrot does try a new

Pieces of corn on the cob are fun to eat—especially when skewered and hung on a vegetable kabob.

food, there is always the chance that it will be accepted and added to the diet.

Many birds will not try new food that is put in a dish but will express interest if the food is offered in a different, more interesting fashion. If you chop up greens in a bowl and your bird doesn't show any curiosity, try hanging uncut greens from a skewer or weaving them through the cage bars. Often this in itself will stimulate the bird to examine and test the offering. You may also try to put some seeds in the bowl underneath the greens and vegetables. The bird will often fling aside the greens to get to the seeds, but at least it is getting a taste of the vegetables and establishing a familiarity with them. Once your parrot overcomes its natural resistance to something new and strange, it will then be able to decide whether the new food is something it can enjoy.

A great way to encourage picky eaters to try foods is to make the new offering a challenge. Even the fussiest of eaters can't resist a challenging game or puzzle. Take a look at the many acrylic food and treat dispensers available to hang in your bird's cage. These hanging dispensers vary from simple food and treat holders to puzzle-type maze toys from which food literally has to be worked out. Rotating the different types of treat holders and dispensers in and out of the cage keeps your picky eater interested and will usually encourage even non-picky birds to more readily try new foods. The added benefit is hours of entertainment—for your bird and for you.

If your parrot is an extremely picky eater, additional vitamins, minerals, or other dietary supplements may have to be added to either the food or the water on a daily basis. However, it is imperative to seek the advice and follow the instructions of a qualified avian veterinarian before supplementing any parrot's diet with added vitamins or minerals. Remember that most birds get an adequate supply of essential dietary needs with a good, varied diet. Furthermore, a picky eater could be the sign of a sick, bored, or otherwise unhappy parrot. An avian veterinarian can conduct an examination to make sure that your parrot is healthy. Once you are confident that it is not suffering from any illness, you can work on finding innovative ways to encourage your picky eater to try—and eventually prefer—a healthy, varied diet.

A balanced diet should provide all of a bird's nutritional needs, but a veterinarian may suggest a mineral block or other supplement.

Grooming and Good Health

O ne of the best ways to ensure the good health of a companion bird is to prevent problems from happening in the first place. A routine that involves regular and thorough cleaning and disinfection, a nutritious diet, plenty of fresh air and sunlight, periodic grooming measures, and frequent bathing or misting can help. Many of these things go hand in hand. Bathing, for example, is one of your greatest allies in the effort to maintain good health and hygiene because it can encourage your bird to take care of many of its other grooming and cleaning needs, such as preening, beak grinding, etc.

Bathing

To a parrot owner, there is perhaps nothing more soothing than watching a pet perform its grooming rituals after a bath. Most birds enjoy a daily misting and will then bask in the relaxing process of drying out and fluffing their feathers. Although many parrots do not initially love bathing, they usually learn to enjoy it over time. However, an owner has to consider each parrot's preference and find the way it enjoys bathing best. This is more important than many companion bird owners realize. Countless people have told me quite emphatically that their birds hate bathing. It is not surprising that several of these owners also admitted to spraying their birds with water as a type of punishment for screaming behaviors. No type of punishment is acceptable with birds. Furthermore, spraying them with water to reprimand them only makes them learn to dislike water and bathing—which, of course, is a very important part of their basic hygiene rituals as well as a necessity for their overall good health.

You are already aware of the importance of providing your avian companion with fresh, clean, uncontaminated drinking water at all times. Because many birds have a tendency to bathe in their

Some birds enjoy bathing in a bowl of water (preferably not its drinking water); others prefer to be misted.

water bowls or to dunk their food in them, it is important to carefully monitor the condition of your bird's drinking water. This may mean using a specially designed drinker or even changing the water bowl several times a day. The value of clean water to your parrot's health cannot be under-estimated.

Wing and Nail Trims

Unless you are experienced in the grooming techniques involved in wing and nail trimming, I encourage you to take your bird to an avian veterinarian or an experienced avian groomer for such procedures. An improperly trimmed nail can result in excessive bleeding. It can also result in the bird's inability to properly grasp or perch. Likewise, improperly trimmed wings can cause a whole host of problems, including excessive bleeding from a cut blood feather. The process can be tricky, and it can vary from bird to bird. Although wings are usually trimmed to prevent birds from

Bathing—and the preening and grooming that follows—is an important and enjoyable part of a bird's life.

being able to fly, they should be long enough to allow a bird to glide to the ground if the need arises rather than dropping like a rock. When wings are cut too short or unevenly, birds cannot fly properly. This is extremely important for those times when a bird will be startled while out on its playstand and instinctively try to fly. An uncontrolled plunge to the ground presents as serious a problem as an uncontrolled flight. Birds can hurt their breastbone, break a beak, or sustain any number of injuries by having wings cut so short that they cannot control even a simple descent. This is why only a professional or someone with serious experience should do the job. Another reason to take your bird to someone else is that often birds will resent, at least initially, the trimming. It is better to let your bird resent the

Birds preen their feathers to keep them clean, in good condition, and properly aligned for flight.

A bird's ears are hidden and protected by a layer of feathers; your vet may examine them during a routine checkup.

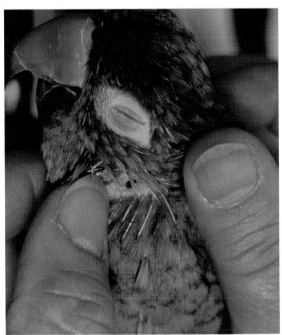

veterinarian and think of you as the one who is there to "rescue" poor Polly.

Undercover

For the sake of overall health, your parrot will also need to be provided with a place where it can receive adequate sleep. Most experts agree that birds probably need at least 10 to 12 hours of sleep per night. This means uninterrupted sleep. A cage cover helps to ensure that your bird feels protected and is surrounded by darkness. There are many types of cage covers available and most feature darker colors that will adequately cut out lighting to ensure privacy. Designer covers can be "personalized" to include your bird's name and picture. If you are a night person or an early riser, take steps to provide your parrot with a location for sleeping that will allow for routine hours of rest regardless of your flexible and changing schedule. Keep in mind that proper lighting during daylight hours is as important to your bird's good health and feather growth as darkness is during the night. Be certain that your parrot has access to natural lighting during daylight hours. Sunlight is always best, but if you do put your bird in the sun, it is critical that you also provide it with a shady area where it can go if the heat gets too intense. Shade should always be available regardless of the outside air temperature—even on a cool day your bird may want to keep out of the sun, and it should always have that option. If natural light from outside is not readily available in your home and you don't often get your birds outside there is another alternative: full spectrum lighting provides the same healthy standards as natural sunlight. It encourages healthy feather growth and allows your bird to enjoy the other benefits of sunlight right from its own indoor cage. Full spectrum lighting has the added benefit of ensuring that your parrot is not in direct, sometimes hot, sunlight, and it also allows you to control the time and number of hours of exposure.

Special Effects

Showers, lighting, trimming, and adequate sleep are essential to basic hygiene and health, but there is much more to grooming Polly. Just as many of us enjoy a trip to the barbershop or beauty salon, birds enjoy a little special treatment in the area of grooming.

A cockatiel's wing before (left) and after (right) trimming. Cockatiels are strong fliers and may need an extra feather or two trimmed.

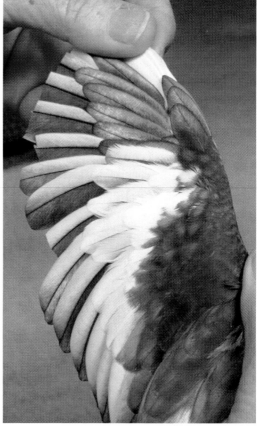

The Proper Wing Clip

When done properly, a wing clip should allow a bird to glide a short distance to the ground and land safely. In other words, the clip should eliminate the possibility of upward flight. Done incorrectly, a clipped bird will not be able to control a fall and may be injured.

Wing clipping can be traumatic for a bird, so many owners prefer to have a professional handle the chore. If you choose to do it yourself, always have a vet, breeder, or groomer show you the procedure the first time. Clipping is a two-person job, so you'll need to find someone to restrain your bird while you do the trimming. You'll also need blunt-nosed scissors, a towel, and styptic powder or cornstarch to be applied in the event that a feather begins to bleed.

The person restraining the bird should wrap it in a towel, with only its wing and face exposed. Gently but firmly hold the bird around the back of the head and hold the lower part of the bird's body. The person doing the trimming should extend the wing, holding the part closest to the bird's body. Examine the primary feathers for any blood feathers (those that have dark blood-filled shafts are still growing and should not be cut). Cut the outer primary flight feathers so that they extend about a half-inch beyond the primary coverts.

The number of feathers you'll need to trim will vary, but it is always better to trim an additional primary flight feather if necessary than it is to cut fewer feathers too short. Start with four, then test the bird indoors, in a carpeted area; if it can still fly upward when it flaps its wings and jumps off your arm or a perch, it needs additional feathers clipped. For example, a heavier Amazon may need four or five trimmed, but a strong-flying cockatiel would need more. Both wings should be clipped evenly; clipping only one results in a loss of control and balance.

BEFORE CLIPPING

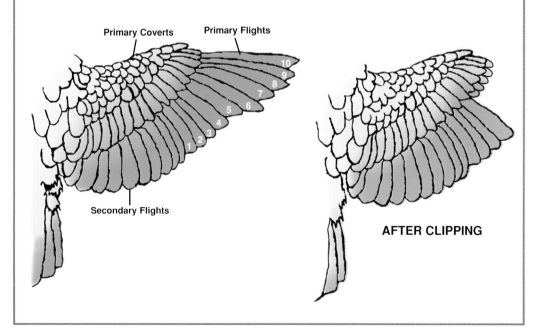

Primary Coverts   Primary Flights

Secondary Flights

AFTER CLIPPING

Many pet stores offer a wide array of health aids and products, but it's best to check with your avian vet before treating symptoms on your own.

Bathing can and should be a fun experience for both you and your bird, thanks to the many products now available to help bird owners pamper their companion parrots. Nonslip shower perches with attachable suction cups allow your bird to take a shower with you if that is a practice you both enjoy. Misters and sprayers are also available for those birds that may enjoy anything from a fine rainforest misting to a torrential downpour. Pressurized plant sprayers are a great way to provide a nonstop shower for your bird either indoors or out. If you house your birds in an outdoor area, check into a mist system, which is something that is usually available at hardware stores. This system of nozzles and tubing attaches to your garden hose and allows you to simulate a rainforest of your own in the size, shape, and area that you need.

After you determine which way your bird likes to bathe best, consider the many products that are available to enhance the experience. Special bird shampoos that are safe for bloody or soiled feathers can be used occasionally when necessary. Other sprays to enhance feather sheen may also be used, although in most cases ordinary tap water is usually the best product you can use to bathe your parrot. In addition, installing a soft water system is a wonderful way to condition the water used in your household, and both you and your parrots will benefit.

One of the best ways to indulge your parrot after a shower is to dry the damp feathers with a hand-held blow dryer. Set the blow dryer on cool only, no heat, and at the lowest blowing speed. Either hold your parrot or allow it to perch on a playstand or perch and begin slowly moving the dryer back and forth across its plumage. Talk or sing to your bird as you begin and tell it how much fun this is. Some birds may be scared or shy at first so observe carefully and don't get too close with the dryer or move too fast. With constant reassurance and gentle handling, your bird will probably overcome any initial fear and welcome the attention it is getting as well as the feeling of having its feathers gently dried. Watch your bird's reaction and you will be able to see if it is enjoying the process. Many birds will fluff up all over and even squeal with delight as they are being dried—especially if the owner appears to be enjoying it too. If you have more than one bird, allow the others to watch as you dry the one that seems to be the least afraid. The others will usually be less afraid after they have observed you or one of their flockmates getting groomed. This will allow you to bathe your companion parrot more often during the long winter months when it could otherwise be too cold to allow it to dry naturally.

Bathing is especially important in the winter when the air in your house is usually drier from heating systems and from being closed up. Proper feather maintenance requires a higher level of humidity than some houses normally provide in the winter, or even at other times during the year—especially houses in the southwestern states. Many bird owners recommend installing a humidifier in the birdroom or in an area of the house where birds are normally kept to assist in keeping the air moist. Those equipped with a filter or an air purifier also help to keep dander down, which can be a real advantage for cockatoo owners.

Although humidifiers work well, you can do even more to enhance your bird's living conditions—and at the same time do something enjoyable for yourself. Consider getting a fountain for the birdroom or for the central location in the house that your birds inhabit. The small indoor desktop fountains are probably not as efficient at raising the humidity in the room as a humidifier. However, if you have the room for it, a large outdoor fountain creatively arranged in a room works great. The fountain not only raises the humidity level but also simulates the soothing sound of a cascading waterfall. Fill the fountain with distilled or filtered drinking water and it will be a safe place for the birds to explore from time to time—under careful supervision, of course. Add bird-safe potted plants and indoor compatible greenery and your birds will be living in the most natural setting you can provide for them within your home. You will also enjoy the beauty and pleasure of having this type of atmosphere right in your own living room. For a more complete effect, try putting on a recording of nature sounds, such as a rainforest or a thunderstorm.

Sunshine benefits a bird's health and spirits, but be certain your bird doesn't get overheated.

Health Issues

Although the range of diseases that can afflict a parrot include some serious and even incurable afflictions, most of them are rare and will require the immediate assistance of a veterinarian. Rather than spend time on those, owners should concentrate most of their energy on everyday concerns and preventative measures.

Foul Water

Contaminated water is one of the greatest health concerns that bird owners should be aware of. Bacteria from food or feces that may fall into a water bowl can seriously undermine your bird's good health. Again, be certain to keep the water in your parrot's bowl clean. This will probably mean changing it several times a day. You may also wish to purchase one of the many styles of domed water and food bowls available at pet stores. These come in easy-to-clean bird-safe ceramic and fit readily into the same holders that regular dishes use. The domed top ensures that droppings or tossed food will not contaminate the water. However, because some birds like to dunk their food, you should still make sure that the water is changed regularly.

Fresh is Best

Do not leave fresh fruits and vegetables in a bird's dish for longer than a few hours. If your bird is outdoors in an aviary or in a warm location, this time limit should be even further reduced. If you pamper Polly with special treats such as hard-boiled eggs, beans, sprouts, and other more delicate foods, be sure to remove them within a few hours of being offered. Sometimes I will offer my birds a homemade treat like those mentioned above, but they will not be in the mood for it at the time. If you notice that your bird is not interested in eating, it is often better to pull the bowl, cover it with plastic wrap, and refrigerate it until later. Most birds will eat their heartiest meals first thing in the morning and again in the early evening, so you can try again then.

Toxic Plants

Poisonous plants can also cause serious harm if ingested, so they should not be anywhere in the house where your bird could inadvertently chew on them. Many other items are extremely harmful to birds: air fresheners, rug deodorizers, and some non-stick cookware. A current list of harmful plants and substances (see Making a House a Home), kept in a handy location, can help you to avoid a potential tragedy.

Do whatever you can to make your bird as safe and comfortable as possible in its home.

Weight Control

One of the best indications of your bird's general good health is its weight. Weigh your birds at least once a month. An accurate digital bird scale with a perch that measures weight in grams is a worthwhile investment. Any noticeable changes in weight should be monitored and you should consult your veterinarian as necessary.

Ailing Feet

Sore or scaly feet are often a problem, especially in older or handicapped birds. Having the proper perches, providing a platform or place for resting the feet, and keeping the house properly humidified can greatly reduce these problems.

Nasal Distress

Blocked or bleeding nostrils can occur and are often caused by allergies or dry air. Some birds will irritate the area by attempting to scratch it with their foot. This can cause bleeding from the nostril. Generally, this is not serious. If you clean the area with fresh water and notice no further bleeding or irritation you can be fairly certain that your bird is fine.

Nail trims are best done with assistance and some previous training; ask your vet or breeder for help.

However, if blocked or bleeding nostrils are a regular occurrence, even after adding moisture to the air, a trip to the avian veterinarian should be seriously considered.

Plumage Concerns

Broken or frayed feathers are often a problem with companion birds. One of the most common reasons is that the bird's wings have been trimmed improperly. Another way for a bird to break feathers is when it is untrimmed and kept in an inadequately sized cage. Usually, if the cage is large and roomy with adequate bar spacing and your bird's wings have been properly trimmed, broken or frayed feathers are not a problem. If you provide these things and still notice that your bird has feather problems, examine the cage and play area to ensure that there are no toys or play things that can cause wing damage. Also, make sure your bird is not indulging in feather picking.

Keep It Trim

Overgrown beaks or nails are another concern with companion birds. Overgrown beaks make it difficult or impossible for your bird to eat properly or even drink water. Long nails can reduce your

First Aid Essentials

The following items should be kept in a convenient location, to be used in the event that you must stabilize your bird enough to be taken to an avian veterinarian. A box will serve the purpose of storing the items, but something sturdy with a handle (like a toolbox) is best.

- The name, phone number, and address of your veterinarian and of the emergency clinic that you use when the vet's office is closed.

- Small travel carrier or hospital cage for keeping your bird secure and for transporting it to the vet.

- Towel for holding or restraining your bird.

- Something to stop bleeding: styptic powder, cornstarch, or flour.

- Bandages: rolls and pads of gauze, plus masking tape for holding pads in place.

- Scissors, tweezers, and needle-nosed pliers for pulling blood feathers.

- Hydrogen peroxide and a disinfectant for cleaning wounds, plus cotton balls and swabs.

- Eyedropper and syringe (with the needle removed) for administering fluids and medication or for irrigating wounds.

- Heating pad for keeping a bird warm in a travel carrier or hospital cage.

- Extra bird food and bottled water; perhaps some kind of glucose solution for restoring lost fluids.

bird's ability to perch properly and they can also get caught on toys, ropes, and cage bars. There is never any reason to allow your bird to live with an overgrown beak or with long nails. In general, most birds will automatically groom themselves properly—you need only to provide them with the means to do so, with items such as concrete perches and wooden toys for chewing. If a bird's beak is misaligned or has some other serious deformity, it will have to be examined by an avian veterinarian. Other than that, most birds will not need to have their beaks trimmed at all. Sometimes nails will have to be trimmed, even with concrete and wooden perches and toys. However, this will have to be done far less often if you allow your birds the means to wear them down naturally, and it is a lot less traumatic for both of you that way.

Safe By Your Side

Many serious health issues are the result of allowing your parrot unsupervised time out of the cage where household hazards abound. Consider purchasing one of the many different types of body perches available so that your parrot can perch comfortably on you while you go about your daily chores. Many of these designs include aprons with an attachable perch that hooks onto the front. Others come equipped with capes that have attached toys and hooks so that you can add or interchange different things to keep your parrot safely occupied while it is spending time with you. Clever designs also protect your clothes from being chewed or soiled. Parrots are naturally curious creatures that like to explore almost everything. You would never consider allowing a two-year-old child to explore everything in the house unattended and you should practice this same caution with your companion birds. In addition to the normal household hazards, there are also increased risks of a bird getting stepped on, flying out of an open door, or getting hurt by another family pet. The list of ways in which your parrot can fall into serious harm is endless. Please exercise caution at all times—and especially when your parrot is out of its cage.

Emergency Response

Although many unfortunate accidents can and should be prevented, it is wise to be prepared for an emergency. Have your avian veterinarian's number readily available, as well as several other emergency numbers as alternatives. Keep a small hospital cage on hand with a heat source, because heat is often an effective treatment for sick birds. You may wish to have a brooder or an incubator available, especially if you have breeding birds. These are usually equipped with automatic temperature regulating systems that can also be used to keep ailing birds warm. If a trip to the veterinarian is warranted, a small cage can be used for transportation; acrylic travel cages work well for this purpose and usually come equipped with a locking door latch for safety during transport.

First Aid First

Finally, have an avian first aid kit on hand at all times. Such a kit should include styptic powder to stop bleeding and droppers for feeding or giving water to ailing birds. It should also have a towel for restraint, cotton swabs and balls, tweezers, scissors, antiseptic wash, and a syringe. Don't wait for an emergency—be prepared ahead of time. It could save your bird's life.

Taming and Training

Though it may sometimes be hard to say who is training whom, the taming and training process can be enjoyed by both you and your parrot. You will discover that the whole process will also help you learn and grow yourself. As an added benefit, once your bird is tamed, it will respond to you enthusiastically; birds usually want to please their human flockmates and will do what they can to gain their approval. From here it is only a small step toward encouraging your bird to perform. Most parrot owners will agree that birds love to put on an act; in fact, they love almost anything that will get them noticed. Regardless of whether you want your bird to talk, sing, perform tricks, or merely obey certain commands, the key is to initiate and follow basic taming and training techniques. In other words, you have to train yourself to train your bird.

Basic Taming and Training Tips

To start, your bird will need to understand and master the basic "step up" command. Before you can begin any sort of training process your bird will need to know how to step up on your finger—or perhaps on a stick at first—and to enjoy doing so. Once you and your bird accomplish this, you can assume that the bird is tame enough that you can begin the process of training.

How you win your bird's confidence and teach it to come to you on command can be done in any number of ways. With the right attitude and preparation, taming and training can be as simple as ABC. I use ABC as a short way of describing the three necessary ingredients that I find work best when attempting to tame or train a new bird: Allowances, Behaviors, and Consistency.

First, make allowances for both of you. Suppose, for example, that you are attempting to tame or train an African Grey parrot. You must realize that you might need to use a different approach with one particular African Grey than you would with birds of a different species or even with a different African Grey. Make allowances for the fact that each bird is an individual. Then, be willing to continuously change your own conduct, techniques, and training methods whenever they do not seem to work with a particular bird. Also, make allowances for the fact that sometimes nothing that you know about or have read about works, and so you must

Playstands are often portable, so your bird can be moved from room to room with you.

not be afraid to try something totally new; entire books are available that are dedicated to taming and training techniques.

Next, be aware of your bird's behavior and try to understand why it does what it does. At the same time, be aware of your own behavior, never forgetting that how you behave is probably the greatest influence on how your bird will behave toward you.

Finally, and most importantly, be consistent in your taming and training techniques. Be consistent in your expectations and in your own actions. Reward your bird consistently for good behavior. And consistently teach your bird to behave the way you would like it to.

Toys and Tricks

Once your bird has been successfully tamed and trained to respond to different commands, the fun really begins. A trip to a local bird shop will definitely be in order. I encourage you to take your feathered companion along and, if the shopkeeper permits, allow your parrot to pick out its own toys and equipment. I have had the most success with the toys and treat dispensers that my own birds have picked out. If they express an interest in the toy, they will be more enthusiastic about working with it.

A tame Gold-capped conure finds a friend in a young boy. Such a relationship can be mutually beneficial.

There are hundreds of toys and accessories available for your bird's entertainment. Small plastic basketballs and hoops, mini skateboards and scooters, and special games such as ring toss are designed especially for parrots to use to perform tricks. Tiny stuffed animals are some of the newest toys to appear on the market for Polly—of course the parrot dolls are the most popular!

Allow your bird a little freedom in deciding which toys it prefers. Birds usually develop strong feelings one way or the other, and they will either love a new toy or hate it. Let your bird decide what it wants to play with. Offer a variety. Your parrot may wish to play basketball one day and ride a skateboard the next. Also, remember that your bird may like a particular toy today but tomorrow could just as easily prefer the one it used to hate. Rotate your bird's toys in and out of the cage and even change training equipment from day to day.

A three-month-old Military macaw gets busy with a new toy. Always make certain toys are safe and non-toxic.

Handfed babies such as these four-week-old cockatiels tend to bond to humans fairly easily.

Stainless steel quick disconnect hangers provide a handy method for quickly interchanging toys on a daily basis. These devices are available at most hardware stores and work well as safety latches on cage doors also. Buy several and install them on all of your hanging toys and treat dispensers so that you just have to unsnap them to interchange things.

Some classic favorite toys are now reappearing in modern fashion. Birds have always enjoyed looking at themselves in a mirror, but today there are small, medium, and large size block mirrors available with six sides of viewing fun; these often come with hanging bells to further entertain your bird. Other toys are constantly being created as people research just what makes their parrots happy. Plastic chains, keys, and log kits are available to entertain as well as teach your parrot how to assemble or recognize shapes, colors, and size. Parrot mobiles have even been designed that can be hung from the top of the cage; some are complete with music to stimulate and soothe your favorite feathered companion with both sight and sound.

Treat dispensers and puzzle toys are also great fun for your bird. You, too, will get hours of enjoyment watching your parrot learn to disassemble a puzzle type toy to get at a treat or just for the fun of it. There are toys that birds can activate to play music and things they can twist to release food. Sample some of these new toys, but don't forget about some of the old standbys: simple blocks of wood and untreated pieces of cardboard or paper are always loved by most birds. Parrots, no matter how tamed and trained they may become, still enjoy simple random acts of destruction! Give them plenty of toys that safely allow them to do just that.

Local bird clubs are a great resource to share ideas and learn how to make your own toys. Other parrot owners will be happy to demonstrate the different toys they make for their companion birds. In time, you will be able to creatively invent various inexpensive toys of your own. You may enjoy making them as much as your parrot will enjoy destroying them.

Learning tools are also available for both you and your parrot. Bird training videos can demonstrate how to teach your parrot certain tricks. There are also videos on a wide variety of avian subjects, ranging from choosing the right bird to correcting behavioral problems. Specialty subjects even assist you in breeding your parrots or in learning proper handfeeding techniques. Your bird can also enjoy and benefit from a number of tapes and videos that are available. Speech training can be greatly enhanced by the use of audiotapes or videos. However, keep in mind that nothing should ever replace the one-on-one training that you and your parrot will engage in when learning anything new or fun.

Activities and Games

Besides routine taming and training, there are loads of fun activities for you and your bird to enjoy. Get creative. Many owners find that their birds really love to play hide and seek. Learn to improvise so that each bird gets to play the game the way it likes best. For example, some parrots love to hide behind one of the toys in the cage and then jump out on one side or the other when you say "peek-a-boo!" Others will fluff up with excitement as they are carried down a hallway and dropped off. Then, as their owner takes off running to hide in another room, these birds

Parrot playthings can be handmade or purchased from stores or catalogs. An eager Amazon checks out a box of goodies and wooden toys.

Toys designed to be shredded may be a good choice for a bird that overpreens or plucks its feathers.

will waddle down the hallway, sometimes shrieking excitedly until they locate their favorite human flock member.

Try holding your parrot on your lap on a towel and then gently lift up a corner of the towel until you are hidden from sight. Lower it and greet your bird enthusiastically, saying "peek-a-boo!" Soon this will become a fun game for you both. There is an even greater reward from the towel game: over time, your parrot will lose its fear of the towel and will instead regard it as part of a fun interactive sport. Birds that are "towel-friendly" are easier to handle in an emergency, when holding them quietly may save their lives. Even routine wing and nail trims are made much easier if your parrot is not afraid to be cradled in a towel. When playing towel games, try to use the same towel each time and choose a color that your parrot seems to like. Use this towel when you have your parrot on your lap cuddling with you as well as during playtime. Once your bird is not afraid of the towel, find one in a similar shape and color to keep with the emergency first aid kit. It may end up being both a comfort and a lifesaver for your parrot.

Time spent bonding with a baby will pay off later with years of love and devotion.

If you're thinking about adding to your avian flock, keep in mind that two parrots are more likely to socialize with each other than with you.

Birds seem to really enjoy being out of their cages, and sometimes they just don't want to stay on their playstands. Try hanging a curly wire-stiffened rope perch from the ceiling and hook some toys to that. You may discover that your parrot enjoys bouncing, swinging, and twirling around on that particular toy. In fact, you may want to hang or otherwise install perches throughout the house. Ceiling swings with hanging acrylic trays beneath them are available so that you can allow your parrot the freedom to perch in any room without fear of making a mess on the floor or carpeting. The trays usually detach for easy cleanup. Your bird will love being around you no matter where you are. There are many different types of portable perches and tabletop playstands that you can purchase and then customize by adding your own toys or treat dishes.

If you carefully supervise your bird at all times, you can allow it some time on the floor, too. Many parrots, especially some species of cockatoos and African Greys, seem to enjoy spending time on the floor. Try gathering up different toys just for this activity—ropes, wood chunks, large nuts in the shell, etc. Then teach your bird to play catch or to fetch a toy and bring it to you. It's quite simple to teach a parrot to pick up pieces of sliced wooden branches and carry them back to you. They usually delight in putting them into your hand and they love when you act thrilled to get them. Many birds love fooling around with slippers—they will often roll around and throw the slipper in the air, looking more like a puppy than a parrot. Tearing up paper is another welcome activity for many birds. Start with clean white paper (avoid newspaper or anything with ink, crayon, or pencil marks), then crumble the paper into a tight ball and toss it to your parrot. They will usually delight in unraveling the paper first and then shredding it to bits. Yes, it can be a little messy, but think of the pleasure it provides to your friend.

Wing flapping should be encouraged because it is a natural behavior that provides exercise for a bird.

The key to having a good time with your bird is first to engage your imagination. If it seems like it could be fun, try it. Don't just stick to traditional bird tricks or training sessions. Learn to recognize what your parrot is capable of doing and what it enjoys doing and then work with that. You may both be surprised at the games you can play and the tricks your parrot can do.

Although it can be more complicated, another often overlooked activity is taking your bird with you to different places whenever possible. I sometimes bring my parrot to an outdoor cafe to meet other bird owners and their parrots. Some owners will let their birds out of their cages, and others use a recently developed type of leash and harness suitable for birds. This system allows the parrot to perch on a shoulder or table and still be restrained without being confined to a cage. Even if you choose the safest method of all, keeping your bird in its small travel cage, you will find that it will still enjoy the sights, sounds, and activity around it.

Discipline Problems and Difficult Birds

In spite of their best efforts, bird owners occasionally find that they are living with a difficult bird that refuses to cooperate with training techniques. Patience is the key to winning these birds over. It is important to remember that, unlike most dogs and cats, birds retain much of their wild instincts. However, they have a tendency to live much longer than dogs and cats, so you have more time to work with them. Patience is perhaps the best-kept secret to establishing satisfying human/avian relationships.

Difficult birds present many types of discipline problems, such as screaming, biting, and refusing the "step up" command. Wise owners approach these birds with patience and consistency. Ideally, owners want their companion parrots to be sweet and loving. So what can be done to help this process along? Fortunately, there are several things that do help owners handle difficult birds and at the same time improve their relationships. Sometimes you may have to indulge Polly with extra attention and treats. But simple changes in routine can often turn difficult birds into well-adjusted companions.

Large parrots such as macaws can destroy a toy in minutes, so try to pick out those toys that are durable.

Increasing exercise and playtime may help a companion parrot to rid itself of excess energy, frustration, and boredom. Try adding more fun activities—such as hide and seek and towel games—to your bird's schedule. Or teach your bird how much fun wing flapping can be. Hold your parrot gently by the toes as it is perched on your finger, or make certain it is holding tightly to a stick if you are using that instead. Gently raise and lower your hand, or the stick, all the while expressing your

If toys, treats, and attention don't work with a difficult bird, a five-minute "time out" in its covered cage may help it settle down.

delight in the activity. This will encourage the bird to flap its wings. This often becomes a treasured game, wonderful exercise, and a great stress reliever for you both!

Never underestimate the calming influence of a bath or shower. It works for you and it will work for your bird. Even the most excitable bird will usually be much more relaxed after it has experienced a soothing bath or shower. An added benefit is that bathing often encourages preening sessions, which will also relax your bird and keep its feathers in top condition.

A difficult bird may be easier to handle when it is placed in a different room away from the cage and living area that it is used to. Many birds become territorial and defend their living areas with vigor, ignoring any and all training efforts to the contrary. However, once they are put in a neutral setting they become much

No matter how well trained you think your bird is, never jeopardize its safety by letting it fly free outdoors.

more cooperative. Likewise, training sessions conducted in a separate room away from the bird's usual living areas are far more successful. Plus, the bird enjoys the mental stimulation of new surroundings.

Another treat and a way to gain your parrot's trust is to take it on what I call daily "walkabouts." Carry your bird from room to room, all the while explaining every little detail, such as "this is the spare bedroom," or "we will have some of our training sessions in here." Be enthusiastic and show your avian companion something new every time you go on such a walk. My birds particularly enjoy visits to

African Greys are sensitive birds that are prone to boredom and plucking; personal interaction and clever toys can be a solution.

the large mirror behind the door of the spare bedroom. What a treat! You will soon find that your bird looks forward to these little outings with you and is far less territorial when you are walking about.

Taking your bird outside with you (following the proper safety precautions), whether to a neighbor's or to the pet store, and giving it new experiences to stimulate its intellect is a great way to curb many problem behaviors and to build a lasting trust between you both. Don't limit yourselves to your own backyard. You may find that Polly enjoys a trip to the local park or outdoor café as much as you do.

Teenage Trouble

Some owners are under the erroneous assumption that as companion parrots mature, they will become sexually aggressive and, if so, will have to be bred. Many parrots do become more aggressive as they mature; however, there are ways to ensure that you do not lose either companionship or control over your single bird in this stage of development. Often it is a temporary testing stage—think of it like living with a normal everyday avian teenager! All that is usually needed during this time is the proper guidance, attention, and patience that you would normally bestow upon any other teenager. Too many companion bird owners, instead of considering other options, immediately decide that the only answer for a parrot going through this particular stage is to find it a mate. Sometimes that works—more often it is a less than satisfactory solution because the owner loses the companionship of a well-loved pet. Another problem to consider is that you could very well end up with two birds at twice the trouble. It is generally far more beneficial to deal with the sexually maturing companion parrot with patience and understanding rather than running out to find it a mate—unless breeding is something that you had in mind from the start.

Traveling With Polly

Traveling with a companion parrot can make a vacation more enjoyable for everyone. Birds, like small children, find fun and excitement in the whole adventure. Their enthusiasm and curiosity can be contagious, and soon everyone is having a wonderful time. Of course, traveling with companion birds is only enjoyable when things go smoothly; this can only happen if you are prepared for both the trip and any emergencies. Fortunately, with the many wonderful amenities available today, it is easy to plan and enjoy a journey with Polly.

On the Road in Style

As always, preparation and the proper equipment will be your keys to success. First, you must start with a suitable travel cage. It will certainly be smaller than the cage your bird is used to at home but do try to make it comfortable and as roomy as possible. There are many styles of cages suitable for traveling. Some are collapsible and can fold up to be carried like a briefcase. Others are made of acrylic and allow your bird an unlimited "open" view, without bars to get in the way. Familiarize your bird with the travel cage before you leave the house. Arrange the cage in a layout similar to your bird's home cage, putting food and water dishes, perches, etc. in similar locations to the already familiar large cage. Allow your bird to spend time in the travel cage while it is located in different rooms in your home. Make sure that you are always close by so your companion parrot doesn't feel abandoned. Always think safety and only outfit your travel cage with non-breakable food and water bowls. Also, pack your bird's favorite foods and treats to take along whenever possible because certain brands of pellets, cereals, or treats may not be available everywhere you happen to travel. Fresh fruits and vegetables can be purchased along the way—try to stick with organic whenever possible and wash them thoroughly before offering them to

On the road again: these lucky birds travel in style, in an RV equipped with large stackable cages.

your parrot. I find it easier to take along or buy bottled water. In short, the less disruption you have to make to your parrot's diet and routine, the smoother the entire trip will be.

Birds will appreciate the comfort and stimulation of a few familiar toys in their cage. Rope toys work best for entertainment because hard plastic toys or bells tend to bang against the sides of the cage when you travel, disturbing both you and the bird. Smooth wooden perches should not be used for travel cages—either a rope perch or a cement perch will provide your bird with better gripping ability.

Make sure to take along several treat dispensers that can be hung in the cage when you reach your destination. Once you are settled, all suitable plastic toys, bells, and swings that your bird enjoys can be installed in the travel cage. Just remember to remove them before heading out on the road again. Also, remember to bring extra paper and cleaning supplies for the travel cage. There are several bird-safe cleaning and sanitizing sprays available for easy cage cleanup. And definitely bring along a cage cover for your bird's privacy and sleeping pleasure if it is used to having the cage covered at home.

To supply your bird with adequate natural lighting, you can buy a single full spectrum bulb that can be installed in any lamp in a hotel room (don't forget to take it with you when you check out!). Take along a spray bottle and a portable shower perch so that you can give your parrot a daily shower—and don't forget the blow dryer!

Your bird will want and need exercise while traveling, especially because it will probably spend more time than usual in a smaller cage than it is accustomed to. Once you are settled for the day, allow your parrot plenty of time out of the cage. Try some wing flapping exercises and do a few "walkabouts." Your bird will also enjoy spending time on a perch or playstand. There are lots of portable and collapsible playstands to choose from. These range from a simple T-stand on a tripod to small tabletop play-gyms. Choose one or several if you have the room. Many of these collapsible stands fold up quite conveniently for easy storage.

Even conures can go camping. With some careful planning and some extra precautions, you can take your pet on vacation.

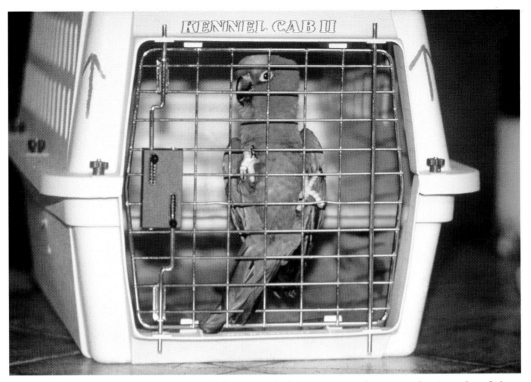

A secure and well-equipped travel cage can safely house your bird during a trip to the vet or to the airport for a flight.

Try to spend as much time with your bird as you can when you are traveling. After all, in many cases you will be the most familiar sight it sees. If your bird has no objections to wearing a lightweight harness, there are a number of them available for your convenience. Some are even equipped with self-containing pouches for droppings. These make outdoor activities with your parrot far more convenient than even a small, lightweight travel cage. It may take your bird some time before it gets used to the idea of wearing a harness, so don't rush it. Make a game out of playing with the harness and allow your bird adequate time to overcome any fear or trepidation. If your bird just does not want to wear a harness, don't force it. As always, if it isn't something enjoyed by your bird, you won't enjoy it either. Consider a lightweight travel cage with a handle or straps instead. The important thing is to contain your bird at all times. Although you may keep its wings properly trimmed, unfamiliar situations can cause a bird to become fearful more easily than when it is in familiar territory. And fear can initiate the natural fight or flight response quickly. Too many birds with trimmed wings have shown unsuspecting owners just how powerfully they can fly when they are frightened—trimmed wings or not. The unfortunate thing is that once a bird does fly off, it becomes even more easily lost in unfamiliar surroundings. So, contain your bird securely at all times when traveling. It can be just as fun in a cage as out on a shoulder—and a whole lot safer!

While you are packing all of the other things to make travel with your parrot easy and fun, don't forget the avian first aid kit in case of an accident or illness on the road. Whether you travel with your parrot or not, you should create a binder with all of your avian companion's vital information, including copies of proof of ownership receipts, DNA paperwork if you have it, and veterinarian records. Make sure to pack this binder whenever your parrot accompanies you on the road. Also, know the regulations that each state or country that you visit has for transporting companion parrots because these do vary quite dramatically. Regulations are constantly changing, so be sure to get the most up-to-date information before you take to the road. It is also a good idea to have a list of the avian veterinarians (see Resources) in each city that you will be visiting as well as in locations along the route. This can be life-saving information in an emergency. Check with your own avian veterinarian because he or she may be able to provide you with a list of names.

A Final Note

All companion bird owners should make provisions for their bird's well-being should they no longer be able to care for it. While you and your parrot are still in good health, check out all the viable options. There are numerous organizations that will take in older, unwanted, or handicapped birds, as well as those whose owners can no longer care for them. Make sure that the organization is reputable and is one conducive to the needs of your parrot. Your local bird club and avian veterinarian can probably give you other options for having your bird taken care of in the event you are no longer able to do so.

Put your instructions in writing and keep copies in the binder that you take with you when traveling with your companion parrot. Using the basic format of a "do-it-yourself" kit for making wills works well for this. Special instructions should also be written down and should list whom the bird is to live with and what other things are to go along with the bird. Whenever possible, make sure that your parrot is familiar with the person who is to provide for it should something happen to you. It is better for both parrot and new owner if they get along. Write down a list of every thing you can think of that will help both your bird and its new caregiver to adapt to each other more easily. Include nicknames, what games the bird enjoys playing, food preferences, and any other information you can think of. Keep the list updated and current. If your bird finds a new toy that it really enjoys, write it down on the list. Include all information and describe things if you need to. For

Outings should be enjoyable for both you and your companion bird, so be certain yours is not stressed by strangers or new situations.

instance, if your bird prefers to bathe in a bowl in the bottom of its cage, write that down. Perhaps another bird you have prefers a misting shower. It is important to spell out each of your bird's specific preferences because this will minimize the already traumatic changes it will have to endure should you no longer be there. Keep an updated copy of these important documents along with all of your companion bird's other vital records readily available for your parrot's new caregiver when the time comes. Include likes and dislikes so the new owner will know just what makes your feathered friend feel the best physically, mentally, and emotionally. Whoever inherits your parrot in the future will probably feel lucky to be gifted with such a wonderful avian companion.

Resources

Bird-Related Websites

www.upatsix.com
www.birdsnways.com

Internet sites feature resources such as chat groups and articles, as well as lists of suppliers, avian associations, breeders, and sanctuaries.

AFA Watchbird

American Federation of Aviculture, Inc.
P.O. Box 56218
Phoenix, AZ 85079
www.afa.birds.org

The AFA is a nonprofit organization dedicated to the promotion of aviculture and the conservation of avian wildlife through the encouragement of captive breeding programs, scientific research, and the education of the general public. The AFA publishes a bi-monthly magazine called *AFA Watchbird.*

Association of Avian Veterinarians

P.O. Box 811720
Boca Raton, FL 33481
561-393-8901
www.aav.org

AAV membership is comprised of veterinarians from private practice, zoos, universities and industry, veterinary educators, researchers and technicians, and veterinary students. Serves as resource for bird owners who are looking for certified avian veterinarians.

Bird Talk

Subscription Dept.
P.O. Box 57347
Boulder, CO 80323
www.animalnetwork.com

Bird Talk is a monthly magazine noted for its directory of avian breeders, as well as its informative articles and columns on health care, conservation, and behavior.

Bird Times

Pet Publishing, Inc.
7-L Dundas Circle
Greensboro, NC 27407
www.birdtimes.com

Bird Times magazine is a source of entertaining and authoritative information about birds. Articles include bird breed profiles, medical reports, training advice, bird puzzles, and stories about special birds.

The Gabriel Foundation

P.O. Box 11477
Aspen, CO 81612
www.thegabrielfoundation.org

The Gabriel Foundation is a nonprofit organization promoting education, rescue, adoption, and sanctuary for parrots.

Midwest Avian Research Expo (MARE)

10430 Dewhurst Rd.
Elyria, OH 44036
www.mare-expo.org

MARE is a nonprofit group dedicated to education and fundraising for avian research projects.

The NAPS Journal

North American Parrot Society, Inc.
P.O. Box 404
Salem, OH 44460
www.drzoolittle.com

Formed in 1995, NAPS sponsors bird shows and aims to put fun back into showing for exhibitors. NAPS members are individual pet owners, breeders with small and large aviaries, show judges, veterinarians, and people who enjoy exhibiting. Members can purchase closed bands from NAPS.

National Animal Poison Control Center/ASPCA
888-426-4435
900-680-0000
In a life and death situation you can call this hotline for 24-hour emergency information. Note: there is a charge for this service.

Pet Bird Report
2236 Mariner Square Drive, #35
Alameda, CA 94501
510-523-5303
www.petbirdreport.com
Parrot behaviorist Sally Blanchard provides information on care and behavior problems, both in her magazine and on her website. Her goal is to help owners have the best companion parrots possible

Index

African Greys .21, 51, 55
Air purifier 39
Avian veterinarian 9, 31, 43, 59, 60
Avocado 29
Bar spacing 11
Bathing .33, 34, 53
Beak grinding 33
Beak trimming 41
Behaviors 46
Bird club 49, 60
Birdaholics 8
Biting 7, 52
Blood feathers 37
Blue parakeet 12
Blue-crown conure 20
Boredom 18, 55
Cage 12, 14
Cage bottom 13
Cage cover 16, 20, 35, 53, 58
Cage grating 14
Cage, home 9
Cage, hospital 43
Cage, stackable 58
Cage setup 11
Cage top 12
Camping 58
Caregiver 60
Ceramic crocks 15, 16
Citrus branches 17, 18
Cleaning supplies 20, 58
Cockatiel 36, 48
Cockatoo 6, 7, 20, 21, 51
Commands 46
Companion birds 5
Conures 8, 58
Dangerous foods 29
Diet 9, 23
Discipline 52
Double Yellow-headed Amazon 28
Ears 35
Emergencies 42
Emotional needs 6
Exercise 11, 15, 23, 52
Fear flight 59
Feather condition 53
Feather plucking 7, 55
Feet ailments 41
First aid .42, 43, 59
Food bowls 16
Food supplies 57

Food treat 7
Foraging 23
Fresh fruits 25, 40
Fresh vegetables 25
Games 49
Gold-capped conure 47
Groomer 34
Grooming 9, 33
Habitat 12
Handfed birds 48
Handraised baby 12
Harness 52, 59
Health 39-43
Health aids 38
Homemade meals .27
Humidifier 39
Indian Ringneck 23
Kabobs 30
Lighting, full-spectrum 36, 58
Maintenance 14
Mental needs 6
Mental stimulation 55
Military macaw 47
Millet spray 12, 29
Mimic 5
Mineral block .25, 31
Mirrors 48
Misting 33
Multiple birds 8, 13, 51
Nail trimming .34, 41
Nasal distress 41
Non-stick cookware 40
Nutrition 23
Older birds 19
Organic produce 25, 57
Outdoor time .55, 60
Pampering 6, 38
Peanut butter 28
Pellets 24
Perches 14
Perches, covered 19
Perches, dowel 15
Perches, easy-to-grip 20
Perches, natural branches 15, 18
Perches, shower 38
Pet stores 38
Physical needs 6
Plant sprayers 38
Platforms, covered .19
Playgym 13, 21

Playpen 14
Playstand .38, 46
Playstand, portable 58
Playstand, tabletop 51
Plumage health 41
Preening 33-35, 53
Privacy 20
Problem behaviors 6
Puzzle games 30
Record-keeping 60
Relationships 5
Roosting tents .19
Rose-breasted cockatoo 8, 13, 15, 19, 27
Safety 42, 54
Scarlet macaw .12
Screaming .7, 52
Seeds 24-25
Sexual maturation 55
Sleep requirements 35
Snacks 28
Socialization 51
Speech training 49
Stainless steel bowls 16
Stainless steel .14
Step up command 45, 52

Sunlight 33, 36, 39
Supplements 26, 31
Taming 45
Toxic plants 17, 40
Toys 6, 46, 47, 50, 53, 55
Toys, rope 58
Toys, shredding 50
Toys, wooden .49
Training 45
Training, videos 49
Travel cage 57, 59
Traveling 57-60
Treat 24
Treat clip 12
Treat dispenser 30, 48, 58
Tricks 46
Umbrella cockatoos 8
Vegetables 40
Water .24, 28, 40
Water bottle 14
Water bowls 16
Water, bottled .58
Weight control 41
Wing flapping 11, 52, 58
Wing trimming 34, 36, 37

Photo Credits

Larry Allan, 7B, 25T, 35T, 46, 51

Susan Chamberlain, 6T, 7T, 12T, 12B, 13B, 16B, 19, 21, 25B, 26, 28B, 29B, 30T, 34B, 39, 40, 47T, 49, 55, 59

Isabelle Francais, 6B, 24T, 24B, 41, 56

Terri Ann King, 14, 15T, 16T, 18, 27, 34T, 50B, 52, 58T, 58B, 60

Rafi Reyes, 4, 8, 10, 13T, 15B, 22, 29T, 30B, 32, 35B, 38, 50T, 53T

John Tyson, 1, 9, 28T, 31, 36, 42, 44, 47B, 48, 53B, 54